Affective

Jacob's Ladder

Grades 4-5

Reading Comprehension Program Social-Emotional Intelligence

Student Workbook Poetry

Joyce VanTassel-Baska, Ed.D., &
Tamra Stambaugh, Ph.D.

PRUFROCK PRESS INC.
WACO, TEXAS

T0392208

Prufrock Press Inc.
P.O. Box 8813
Waco, TX 76714-8813
Phone: (800) 998-2208
Fax: (800) 240-0333
http://www.prufrock.com

Table of Contents

Success Is Counted Sweetest 2

Mending. 5

The Fool's Song 9

Casey at the Bat. 12

A Lazy Day 17

Winter Branches 20

From a Bridge Car 22

Success Is Counted Sweetest

By Emily Dickinson

Success is counted sweetest
By those who ne'er succeed.
To comprehend a Nectar
Requires sorest need.
Not one of all the Purple Host
Who took the Flag to-day,
Can tell the definition
So plain, of Victory
As he defeated, dying,
On whose forbidden ear
The distant strains of triumph
Break, agonizing clear.

SUCCESS IS COUNTED SWEETEST

Reflecting on Patterns of Achievement

K3 The character (one of the "purple Host") in Dickinson's poem dies in the final stanza even as he defeats the enemy. What qualities has he exhibited? Would you ascribe success to his action? Why or why not?

_____

_____

_____

_____

_____

_____

_____

_____

_____

_____

_____

_____

_____

_____

_____

_____

Assessing Strengths and Interests

K2 What assets might we infer were employed to defeat the enemy? Is the use of force ever not justified if it brings a desirable outcome? Debate with your partner.

Identifying Barriers to Achievement

K1 What barriers do soldiers face in battle? Make a list of at least 10, half under the heading "physical" and the other half under the heading "mental" and then list the top three. Discuss with your partner why you have more in one column than the other.

SUCCESS IS COUNTED SWEETEST

Demonstrating High-Level Performance in a Given Area

L3 Some people have stated that to be successful, one must have a deep personal need that requires fulfilling. How does the first stanza of the poem view success? What is your view on this issue? Take a stand that defines the criteria you apply to being successful and defend it, using your understanding of the poem and circumstances you have encountered in life.

_____

_____

_____

_____

Applying Learning to Practice

L2 What are the steps to take in becoming successful in a battle, do you think? In life? What is Dickinson's view of the process? How does one become a hero in our culture?

_____

_____

_____

_____

Recognizing Internal and External Factors That Promote Talent Development

L1 What is success? How is it attained? These are questions of interest to everybody at different stages of development. Describe what success looks like to you in a brief statement. What object or symbol would you say most signifies success for you? Why?

_____

_____

_____

_____

Mending

By Hazel Hall

Here are old things:
Fraying edges,
Ravelling threads;
And here are scraps of new goods,
Needles and thread,
An expectant thimble,
A pair of silver-toothed scissors.
Thimble on a finger,
New thread through an eye;
Needle, do not linger,
Hurry as you ply.
If you ever would be through
Hurry, scurry, fly!
Here are patches,
Felled edges,
Darned threads,
Strengthening old utility,
Pending the coming of the new.
Yes, I have been mending . . .
But also,
I have been enacting
A little travesty on life.

Discuss the following aspects of the poem with a partner before beginning the ladders provided:

- What is "a travesty" that the poet mentions in the last line of the poem? What does she mean?

- What are the words in the poem that relate to the act of sewing? Make a list of them.

- How does the act of sewing accommodate new and old things?

- Why does the sewing take on the feeling of urgency? What in life is urgent?

- How is mending (or sewing) in the poem a metaphor for life? What examples support your ideas?

MENDING

Reflecting on Patterns of Achievement

K3 Many people allow life to just happen to them serendipitously. Others plan for specific occurrences. How do you think about your future? Assuming you want to plan for your formal education as a prelude to a career, what are the markers that you would want to experience? Develop an educational plan that begins where you are now and takes you into a professional career. Use the template provided below to "sew in" the relevant pieces and reflect on the pattern you create:

Level	Key Events	Skills I Want to Develop	Accomplishments
Elementary School			
Middle School			
High School			
College			
Career			

Assessing Strengths and Interests

K2 What do you perceive to be your major strengths and areas for improvement? Make a list and describe how your strengths might be used to improve your weaknesses.

_____

_____

_____

Identifying Barriers to Achievement

K1 What barriers would keep you from sewing the life that you might like? Name three and think about how they might be overcome.

_____

_____

_____

MENDING

Demonstrating High-Level Performance in a Given Area

L3 In what ways does the poet relate the idea of creating a life to the act of sewing? In a chart, show what the relationship might be.

Creating a Life	Act of Sewing

Then, create a collage that "sews together" the pieces of your life to date. What might your collage look like in 10 years? Compare and contrast each version.

Applying Learning to Practice

L2 How can the factors from L1 work together to help you achieve your dreams? For example, how can the quality of persistence be applied to your education? Write an essay on a separate sheet of paper that integrates at least three of the factors and describes how they fit together.

Recognizing Internal and External Factors
That Promote Talent Development

L1 What are the factors that you would "sew into your life" that might aid you in developing your abilities and aptitudes to optimal levels? Select from the following list and note how they might aid you.

Factors	How They Are Useful?
Parents	
Motivation levels	
Friends	
Persistence	
Positive outlook (optimism)	
Determination	
Education	
Life experiences (e.g., travel, living in different places)	

The Fool's Song

By William Carlos Williams

I tried to put a bird in a cage.
O fool that I am!
For the bird was Truth.
Sing merrily, Truth: I tried to put
Truth in a cage!
And when I had the bird in the cage,
O fool that I am!
Why, it broke my pretty cage.
Sing merrily, Truth: I tried to put
Truth in a cage!
And when the bird was flown from the cage,
O fool that I am!
Why, I had nor bird nor cage.
Sing merrily, Truth: I tried to put
Truth in a cage!
Heigh-ho! Truth in a cage.

THE FOOL'S SONG

Using Emotion

E3   Why is the phrase *caged truth* an oxymoron (i.e., a two-word contradiction in terms, such as *clearly confused, act naturally, open secret*)? What other oxymorons come to mind that could be applied to create an emotion in the poem? Create one and describe why it might be effective.

_____

_____

_____

_____

_____

Expressing Emotion

E2   Rewrite the poem to reflect another feeling, caused by the same series of events. What emotion have you portrayed, and how has it changed the poem?

_____

_____

_____

_____

_____

Understanding Emotion

E1   The poet expresses emotions about his act. What emotions does he feel about himself and why?

_____

_____

_____

_____

_____

THE FOOL'S SONG

Creating a Plan for Management

J3   How might the poet have better managed the concept of truth than by making it a bird and putting it in a cage? What would you have done? Create your own image of truth and how you would represent it.

Applying Stress Control Techniques

J2   How might the stress portrayed in the poem have been avoided? What measures can you take to avoid stressful situations or reduce them?

Identifying Conditions/Situations That Cause Stress

J1   What stress is the narrator of the poem feeling? What evidence supports your answer? What factors cause stress in your life? What kinds of situations do you experience as stressful?

Casey at the Bat
By Ernest Lawrence Thayer

The outlook wasn't brilliant for the Mudville nine that day;
the score stood four to two, with but one inning more to play.
And then when Cooney died at first, and Barrows did the same,
a sickly silence fell upon the patrons of the game.

A straggling few got up to go in deep despair. The rest
clung to that hope which springs eternal in the human breast;
they thought, if only Casey could get but a whack at that—
they'd put up even money, now, with Casey at the bat.

But Flynn preceded Casey, as did also Jimmy Blake,
and the former was a lulu and the latter was a cake,
so upon that stricken multitude grim melancholy sat,
for there seemed but little chance of Casey's getting to the bat.

But Flynn let drive a single, to the wonderment of all,
and Blake, the much despised, tore the cover off the ball;
and when the dust had lifted, and the men saw what had occurred,
there was Jimmy safe at second and Flynn a-hugging third.

Then from five thousand throats and more there rose a lusty yell;
it rumbled through the valley, it rattled in the dell;
it knocked upon the mountain and recoiled upon the flat,
for Casey, mighty Casey, was advancing to the bat.

There was ease in Casey's manner as he stepped into his place;
there was pride in Casey's bearing and a smile on Casey's face.
And when, responding to the cheers, he lightly doffed his hat,
no stranger in the crowd could doubt 'twas Casey at the bat.

Ten thousand eyes were on him as he rubbed his hands with dirt;
five thousand tongues applauded when he wiped them on his shirt.
Then while the writhing pitcher ground the ball into his hip,
defiance gleamed in Casey's eye, a sneer curled Casey's lip.

And now the leather-covered sphere came hurtling through the air,
and Casey stood a-watching it in haughty grandeur there.
Close by the sturdy batsman the ball unheeded sped—
"That ain't my style," said Casey. "Strike one," the umpire said.

From the benches, black with people, there went up a muffled roar,
like the beating of the storm-waves on a stern and distant shore.
"Kill him! Kill the umpire!" shouted someone on the stand;
and it's likely they'd have killed him had not Casey raised his hand.

With a smile of Christian charity great Casey's visage shone;
he stilled the rising tumult; he bade the game go on;
he signaled to the pitcher, and once more the spheroid flew;
but Casey still ignored it, and the umpire said: "Strike two."

"Fraud!" cried the maddened thousands, and echo answered fraud;
but one scornful look from Casey and the audience was awed.
They saw his face grow stern and cold, they saw his muscles strain,
and they knew that Casey wouldn't let that ball go by again.

The sneer is gone from Casey's lip, his teeth are clenched in hate;
he pounds with cruel violence his bat upon the plate.
And now the pitcher holds the ball, and now he lets it go,
and now the air is shattered by the force of Casey's blow.

Oh, somewhere in this favored land the sun is shining bright;
the band is playing somewhere, and somewhere hearts are light,
and somewhere men are laughing, and somewhere children shout;
but there is no joy in Mudville—mighty Casey has struck out.

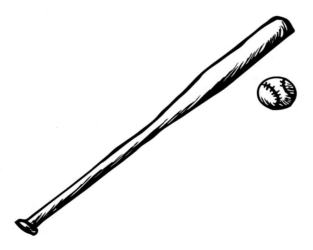

CASEY AT THE BAT

Creating a Plan for Management

J3 What should Casey do next? How should he handle his strikeout? Tell a classmate your thoughts. Then complete the chart below by reframing negative reactions into something positive and productive. An example has been provided for you.

Negative Reaction	Productive Reframe
I have let everyone down.	I have a great hitting record, but missed that one. I will keep practicing.
You knew better than to swing at that pitch.	
You are no longer a good ball player.	

Applying Stress Control Techniques

J2 Reread the four lines of the poem beginning with "There was ease in Casey's manner as he stepped into his place." Was Casey overconfident? Why or why not?

How might Casey's self-confidence help him manage the stress of his situation both before going to bat and after he struck out? Write a true statement about how self-confidence can play a role in stress management. Consider using some of the following words in your statement: success, confidence, belief, stress, failure, anxiety, or perfectionism.

_____

_____

_____

_____

_____

_____

_____

Identifying Conditions/Situations That Cause Stress

J1 What about Casey's situation might cause you stress? If you were in this situation, would your stress be more about trying to live up to other people's expectations or not meeting your own personal goals? Compare your ideas with that of a classmate.

_____

_____

_____

_____

_____

_____

_____

CASEY AT THE BAT

Demonstrating High-Level Performance in a Given Area

L3   Is Casey a great player? What evidence in the poem supports your answer? What criteria would/did you use to judge? Conduct a quick debate with your class.

Applying Learning to Practice

L2   What lesson can be learned from this poem about elite players and their performance? About self-confidence?

_____

_____

_____

_____

_____

_____

_____

_____

Recognizing Internal and External Factors That Promote Talent Development

L1   What factors contributed to Casey's success as a batter? How might one's strength also be his or her weakness? Use evidence from the poem to support your answer.

_____

_____

_____

_____

_____

_____

_____

_____

A Lazy Day

By Paul Laurence Dunbar

The trees bend down along the stream,
Where anchored swings my tiny boat.
The day is one to drowse and dream
And list the thrush's throttling note.
When music from his bosom bleeds
Among the river's rustling reeds.

No ripple stirs the placid pool,
When my adventurous line is cast,
A truce to sport, while clear and cool,
The mirrored clouds slide softly past.
The sky gives back a blue divine,
And all the world's wide wealth is mine.

A pickerel leaps, a bow of light,
The minnows shine from side to side.
The first faint breeze comes up the tide—
I pause with half uplifted oar,
While night drifts down to claim the shore.

A LAZY DAY

Using Emotion

E3   Rewrite the poem on a separate sheet of paper, using your own images and feelings as the basis. What will you title it? Why?

_____

_____

_____

_____

Expressing Emotion

E2   Think about a time when you have had similar feelings as those portrayed in the poem. Describe that time, event, and other aspects of the situation that helped develop your feelings. Make your description as powerful in the use of emotional language as Dunbar has done.

_____

_____

_____

_____

Understanding Emotion

E1   Write down descriptive words (individual and phrases) that Dunbar uses to depict the scene. What feelings emerge as you enter the poet's world? In a second column, make a list of words that describe your feelings about the poem.

Poet's Words	Feelings Conveyed

A LAZY DAY

Creating a Plan for Management

J3   Create a model plan for stress reduction, based partly on your reading of the poem and ideas you get from it, but also from other sources. What stress reducers would you include in your plan? Be sure to read three other sources about how to manage stress.

_____

_____

_____

_____

_____

Applying Stress Control Techniques

J2   What additional choices in activities might you make to further reduce stress?

_____

_____

_____

_____

_____

Identifying Conditions/Situations That Cause Stress

J1   The poet has presented a scene that is often seen to reduce and remove stress. What aspects of the poem appear to be an antidote to stress? Make a list and share with your partner.

_____

_____

_____

_____

Winter Branches

By Margaret Widdemer

When winter-time grows weary, I lift my eyes on high
And see the black trees standing, stripped clear against the sky;

They stand there very silent, with the cold flushed sky behind,
The little twigs flare beautiful and restful and kind;

Clear-cut and certain they rise, with summer past,
For all that trees can ever learn they know now, at last;

Slim and black and wonderful, with all unrest gone by,
The stripped tree-boughs comfort me, drawn clear against the sky.

WINTER BRANCHES

Using Emotion

E3 There are many poems and paintings about nature, including this one. Why might this be? What is it about nature that evokes emotion, do you think? Create a statement about nature that reflects your views on its relationship to emotion.

_____

_____

_____

_____

_____

_____

Expressing Emotion

E2 Apply the poet's feelings to another scene in nature that you create and describe. Write a poem or an essay, paint a picture, or compose or select a piece of music that conveys that feeling, using deliberate techniques to convey emotion. Be prepared to share your piece and explain the techniques you used and what these symbolized (i.e., contrasting colors, shading, personification, tempo, rhythm, metaphors, etc.)

Understanding Emotion

E1 Why is the narrator comforted by the sight of the "stripped tree boughs"? What feelings do they produce in her? What aspects of the trees produce positive feelings? Identify those words or phrases.

_____

_____

_____

_____

_____

From a Bridge Car

By Elias Lieberman

River inscrutable, river mysterious,
    Mornings or evenings, in gray skies or blue,
Thousands of toilers in gay mood or serious,
    Workward and homeward have gazed upon you.

Swirling or sluggish, but ever inscrutable,
    Sparkling or oily, but never the same;
You, like the city, mysterious, mutable,
    Tremble with passions which no one can name.

FROM A BRIDGE CAR

Using Emotion

E3 The river is personified by the poet in this poem, meaning it is given human characteristics and behaves as a human being. Provide evidence from the poem to support that claim.

Create a poem about an aspect of nature and use personification as Lieberman has in this poem to describe it. Now draw the image of nature you have created and give both the poem and the picture a title. What have you selected and why?

_____

_____

_____

_____

_____

Expressing Emotion

E2 Identify words or phrases used by the poet to express the narrator's emotion about the river. What are the feelings? What does the river symbolize?

_____

_____

_____

_____

_____

Understanding Emotion

E1 Identify the most powerful words used to describe the river. What characterization do they provide? How do they make you feel?

_____

_____

_____

_____

_____